Timeless Wisdom on Finance

Timeless Wisdom on Finance

ANIL
LAMBA

Bestselling author of
Romancing the Balance Sheet

HARPER
BUSINESS

An Imprint of HarperCollins *Publishers*

First published in India by Harper Business 2024
An imprint of HarperCollins *Publishers*
4th Floor, Tower A, Building No. 10, Phase II, DLF Cyber City,
Gurugram, Haryana – 122002
www.harpercollins.co.in

2 4 6 8 10 9 7 5 3 1

P-ISBN: 978-93-6213-071-6
E-ISBN: 978-93-6213-654-1

Typeset in 9.3/11.6 Neue Frutiger World at
HarperCollins *Publishers* India

Printed and bound at
Thomson Press (India) Ltd

Dedicated to all the readers of my earlier books, who regularly send extremely kind and encouraging messages, inspiring me to take my work forward with greater enthusiasm.

Preface

The subject of finance management almost always touches a nerve and evokes huge interest, cutting across industry and geographical segments.

My book *Romancing the Balance Sheet*, first published in 2010, continues to receive messages almost daily from readers across the world, spanning various backgrounds and age groups, about how they have benefited and the impact it has had on them.

Seeing their interest in the subject, a few years ago, I began the practice of sending weekly musings on finance management—crisp, succinct snippets—to a select group of friends and readers. They then started forwarding these musings among their social groups and professional colleagues, and the number of recipients grew exponentially.

From time to time, I would receive requests and suggestions to compile these musings in one place, creating an invaluable repository of financial knowledge and wisdom.

That is how this book, which you are now holding in your hands, was born.

The musings are not verbose, but the message each delivers is deep. You will probably find an answer to whatever finance management-related issue or problem you may be facing in one of these extremely thought-provoking capsules.

To benefit from this book, read every nugget more than once, then chew and ruminate over it for the rest of the day.

The more you ponder, the more angles you will discover, and the more sense it will make.

I hope you enjoy reading the book.

Anil Lamba
anil@lamconschool.com
July 2024

Contents

01 Financial Management

02 Accounting

03 Stock Market Investing

04 Income Tax

05 Macro Economics

06 Shorts

Financial Management

Section 01

01. What business are you in

Tata Motors is not in the business of manufacturing automobiles.

Infosys is not in the business of making software.

The Marriott Group is not in the business of providing hospitality-related services.

All these entities are in the same business—one of making profit.

The means vary, the objective is the same.

02. How much money should a business raise

When a business needs money, it has only one option, and that is to borrow.

It borrows from the owners, and it borrows from outsiders.

The former is called capital and the latter is called a loan.

One of the crucial decisions an entrepreneur has to make in the early stages of the business is related to the quantum of funds that should be raised.

Should a business raise more money than needed or less?

If it raises less, it will not be in a position to acquire all the assets required for its smooth functioning, and it will get into trouble. If it raises more money than required, it will get into bigger trouble.

Many businesses sow the seeds of sickness even before the business commences because they either raise less money than required or they raise more.

How much money to raise is a matter of art. It cannot be an arbitrary decision.

03. The secret behind Mr Dhirubhai Ambani's success

Mr Dhirubhai Ambani, in my opinion, is the biggest financial genius India has produced.

What was the reason for his success?

Reliance started manufacturing textiles (remember '**Only Vimal**'?) in the mid-seventies and within a few years overtook its rival, Bombay Dyeing.

Can anyone, by any stretch of imagination, say that in those few years, Dhirubhai's weaving skills had become better than the Wadia family's, which had been in the business for almost a hundred years then?

The reason for his success was his financial sense.

Those who neglect arming themselves with financial management skills do so at their own peril.

Section 01

04. Always remember this mantra

'Less is bad, more is worse.'

'**Less**' reflects shortages, delays, inefficiencies.
'**More**' indicates it is a non-performing asset (NPA).

NPAs are a heavy burden to bear, since they don't earn but the sources that fund these assets continue to cost, and the performing assets (PAs) have to work harder to compensate.

One has to run faster and faster, but on a treadmill.

05. Two pillars of success

Successful businesses stand on two pillars:

1) ability to generate profit
2) ability to effectively manage cash flow

Take care of these two pillars, and most other things will take care of themselves.

And the responsibility for both rests with those who often (mistakenly) call themselves 'non-finance persons.'

06. Learn to read financial statements

Finance is the language which businesses speak.

Problems don't become big overnight. These are small in the beginning and grow gradually.

Those who don't understand the language do not know what their business is trying to communicate through its financial statements.

Such people realize their business is in trouble only when it is too late to do anything to set it right.

Learn to speak and understand the language.

07. Making profit can be dangerous

When an organization makes profit, there are several claimants to it:

- employees (for bonus),
- the government (for income tax)
- the shareholders (for dividends)

To meet the myriad expectations, organizations need money.

However, profit and cash are two different things.

Often, the more the profit a business earns, the lower is its bank balance.

Herein lies the conundrum.

An inability to meet the expectations of any of the three claimants has it repercussions.

08. Are employees assets

A question I'm asked by many an employee is 'Why does my name not appear on my company's balance sheet as an asset?'

To this, my counter-question is, 'Tell me, if you purchase a car, where will you show the cost of the car?'

'It will appear as an asset on the balance sheet' says the employee.

'And if the car has been hired instead, where will you show the hire charges?'

'As an expense on the P&L statement.'

My next question then is, 'Has the company purchased you, or have your services been hired?'

I rest my case.

09. What constitutes finance management

Is a decision to sell at a certain negotiated price (**taken by a salesperson in the field**) a sales decision or a financial decision?

Is a decision to purchase a certain quantity of raw material (**taken by the purchase manager**), so that it suffices the production requirements, purely a purchase decision or does it have a financial implication which must be understood?

Is a decision about the number of people to be recruited and the terms offered (**taken by a human resources [HR] person**) merely an HR decision or does it have financial ramifications too?

Not a single one of these decisions should be taken without a clear understanding of its impact on the organization's bottom line and its cash flow.

And all these departments, paradoxically, call themselves non-finance.

The truth is, more finance management (or mismanagement) happens outside the finance department than inside.

Section 01

10. How to become a financially literate organization

If an organization's production skills are weak, what will it strengthen? The production department.

When it is weak in sales, it will improve the sales department.

If it wishes to improve the quality of its HR, it will strengthen the HR department.

So when an organisation realizes the critical importance of finance management, it will naturally tend to strengthen the finance department.

In my opinion, they are treating the symptom.

Why do I say so?

I say so because finance management does not happen only in the finance department. Finance management or mismanagement happens across the organization in every action of every individual.

If you wish to create a financially intelligent organization, you will have to ensure that financial literacy percolates across every strata of your organization.

11. The term 'non-finance person' is an oxymoron

An action taken after evaluating its impact on the organization's bottom line and its impact on the cash flow is a financially intelligent action.

An organization's finance management is the result of financially intelligent decisions taken by a majority of its employees.

Any person whose actions impact the bottom line and/or the cash flow can never be called a 'non-finance person'.

12. The finance function is an orphan

Section 01

The real finance people call themselves 'non-finance'. (The 'real' finance people being those whose actions can generate profit—the persons in charge of sales, production, procurement, recruitment et al.)

And the finance professionals are not there when finance management or mismanagement is happening.

They come into the picture later, do a post-mortem, and determine whether the organization has made a profit or a loss.

The most neglected function within most organizations is the finance function.

13. Every manager is a finance manager

If I had it my way, I would change the nomenclature of employees' designations.

The marketing manager's designation should read **'marketing-cum-finance manager'**

The vice-president of production should be described as **'vice-president: production-cum-finance'**

The materials manager should be called **'materials-cum-finance manager'.**

Now all of them would effectively be saying they are responsible for taking financially intelligent decisions relating to their domain.

And those who think and say they are 'non-finance' people are actually washing their hands of the financial implication of their actions.

14. When do businesses make profit

A business is composed of a collection of individuals. Its finance management is the result of financially intelligent decisions taken by the individuals running it.

A business makes a profit when the value of financially intelligent decisions outweighs the value of financially deficient ones.

Vice versa, it makes a loss.

15. Definition of success

A business can be termed a success only if the returns generated exceed the cost of the capital employed.

Capital employed includes both the outsiders' as well as the owners' contribution.

There are many who wrongly consider owners' contribution to be free money. And, therefore, their concept of cost of capital and the consequent target of the returns expected is warped.

16. Financial literacy for nation-building

Section 01

A nation made up of poor individuals cannot be prosperous.

For a country to flourish, its people must be financially stable.

An essential ingredient for nations to achieve financial stability is financial literacy.

Organizations manned with financially literate employees are more successful.

Individuals who understand finance management are better-off than those who don't.

There is no substitute for financial literacy.

17. The cost of financial illiteracy

Financial illiteracy can harm a business, cause losses and even result in business closure.

Don't wait to suffer the consequences of financial mismanagement.

It's too late to learn to swim when one is about to drown.

18. Financial literacy is a must

I never cease to marvel at business owners who take a myopic view when it comes to spending money on making their employees financially literate.

The truth is, of the myriad takeaways for anyone who attends a programme on finance management, even if *one* of the learnings is implemented, the benefit to the organization would far exceed the investment made.

And by denying them this knowledge, the continued loss to the organization (about which it is blissfully ignorant) is even greater.

'Penny wise and pound foolish' aptly sums up this attitude.

19. Cash is king

Both profitability and cash-flow management are equally important for a business to be successful. However, during recessions and downturns, profitability takes a backseat and managing cash flow becomes more important.

This is because during such times, profitability of almost everybody is hurt, but the organizations that go under are the ones where cash runs dry.

It becomes essential to explore every avenue to generate, preserve and conserve cash. One must re-negotiate terms with customers, vendors and bankers, notwithstanding what was agreed upon earlier. One must defer, wherever possible, discretionary spends and shelve all new projects which do not bring a certain minimum profitability.

Organizations that are sitting on a pile of cash during recessions can actually be considered 'kings', since recessions also bring opportunities.

There are some wonderful companies available to be taken over at throwaway prices during such times. But in most cases there is no money available to benefit from these opportunities.

20. The two golden rules of good finance management

Section 01

One: Invest only after ensuring that assets can generate a return equal to or greater than the corresponding cost of capital.

Two: Ensure that assets bring a cash inflow before the liabilities demand an outflow.

21. The essence of good finance management

The essence of good finance management lies in the ability to understand

- how much money to raise, from where (equity vs debt) and at what cost;
- where and how much to deploy (between long-term investments and working capital) and the returns to be targeted.

22. Ensure all money does not get exhausted in infrastructure

A large portion of the money raised by a business gets invested in the acquisition of infrastructure.

Care should be taken, however, to ensure that all the money does not get so invested.

Having created infrastructure, businesses must ensure there is money left over, because they will now require a continuous supply of working capital.

23. For whose benefit is a business run

You must have often heard a statement that a business is run for the benefit of all the stakeholders.

I beg to differ.

I think the single objective of running a business is to generate profit for one stakeholder and that is the owner.

The other stakeholders—the vendors, the employees, the lenders—are facilitators in the process.

In the interest of sustainability, it is critical for the facilitators to understand this and to collectively ensure that the owners make profit.

If merely the facilitators are earning and the owners are not, it will be a matter of time before the owners will discontinue the business and then nobody will make money.

24. What defines a financially sound business

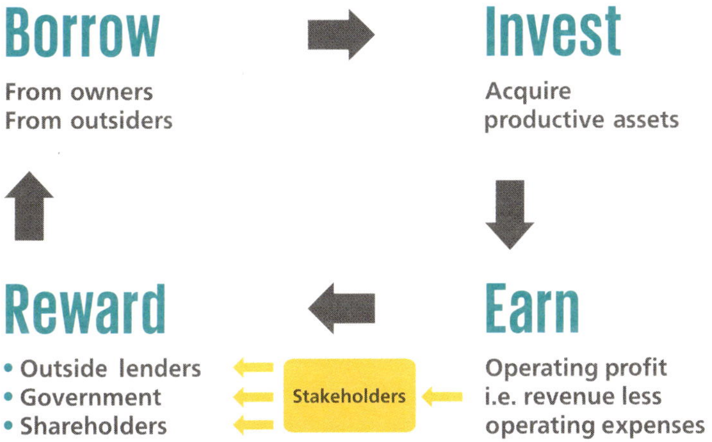

If any of the stakeholders does not get rewarded, or if the order of rewarding is not followed, there will be problems.

25. Gross profit vs net profit ratios

A marginal improvement in the gross profit ratio is a major achievement. A substantial jump in the net profit ratio may not be anything to write home about.

Improvement in gross profit reflects efficiency, better margins, being able to buy/produce more efficiently, being able to command better prices for your products/services.

Even a slight improvement needs substantial effort.

On the other hand, net profit can go up exponentially by doing nothing.

When revenues increase, some costs increase proportionately while others remain fixed, leading to a disproportionate increase in net profits.

No credit goes to efficiency. There is no need to pat one's back.

26. To borrow or not to borrow

Presence of fixed costs in the costing structure result in an exponential impact on the bottom line due to a certain change in the top line. This phenomenon is called the leverage effect.

Leverages work in your favour when sales are on the ascendant and against you when sales start dipping.

Leverages are of two types

1. operating (caused by the presence of operating fixed costs)
2. financial (caused by financial fixed cost, i.e., interest).

The latter are more in control (since to borrow or not to borrow is a choice), while the former are a given (being dependent of the nature of activity).

Organizations with low operating leverages may use borrowed funds to support expansion and growth.

However, those with high operating leverages would do well to opt for equity, else the combined leverage will make the organization extremely risky.

27. Why is leveraging frowned upon

Why are highly leveraged companies looked at with suspicion?

Leverage is a positive word. It is derived from an engineering term called 'lever'. Its function is to provide magnification.

Colloquially, in a financial context, leverage merely refers to using borrowed funds to finance operations. Financial leverage helps in accelerating profit.

To lift a weight, if one takes the help of a lever, the effort exerted at one end is less and the weight that gets lifted at the other end is more.

Similarly, with the help of financial leverages, a small increase in the sales turnover can lead to an exponential increase in profit.

In engineering, a lever works on the principle of fulcrum.

In finance, the fixed cost in the form of interest to be paid on debt acts as the fulcrum.

28. Is leveraging bad

Leveraging per se is not bad. In fact, it helps organizations to exceed their reach beyond their grasp. The problem lies with unproductive and foolish borrowing.

Borrowing is bad if:

1. the borrowed funds are used for unproductive purposes and for acquiring non-performing assets
2. on deploying the borrowed capital, the organization is unable to earn even equal to the cost of borrowing
3. if the utilization of borrowed funds cannot generate sufficient cash inflows to meet the repayment obligations

If the above conditions are not violated, if the borrowed capital can be deployed productively, if the organization can earn greater than the interest payable and if it can ensure that cash inflows are more than sufficient to meet repayment obligations, then the more an organization borrows, the more it will prosper.

29. Cost of equity

It is essential for business owners to recognize equity as a very expensive form of debt.

Understand that the money contributed by the owners has a cost that needs to be recovered from the revenue generated. Treat it with the same respect that is accorded to debt. Recognize the need to preserve and grow it.
Then and only then equity as a source of funding becomes viable.

Once that is understood, whether to raise money through equity or debt simply becomes a trade-off between the lower cost of debt and the loss of control by diluting equity.

30. ESOPs can be dangerous for the organization

I'm all for ESOPs, except those given to the top management, who, in my opinion, should be insulated from the stock market.

When the senior-most personnel—the CEO, the executive director and such—have a vested interest in the market price of the company's stock, then there is a strong urge to ensure the financial statements reflect the market and the analysts' expectations, leading to Enron-type cases.

The market should reflect what the financial statements reveal and not reveal what the market expects.

31. Finance management principles to live by

Ensure that

1. investment in assets generates a return that is at least equal to the cost of capital

2. assets bring a cash inflow before the liabilities demand an outflow

Maintain your

1. current ratio at around 2:1

2. liquid (or quick) ratio at a minimum of 1:1

Never

1. use short-term funds to acquire long-term assets

2. sell your product at negative contribution

Always remember the mantra 'less is bad; more is worse'

Section 01

32. How much should the debt-equity ratio be

When people ask me 'How much is a healthy debt-to-equity ratio?', my answer is, 'the higher the better'.

Equity is expensive money, debt is cheaper.
If a business can afford equity, it can certainly afford debt.

The problem is not with debt per se; it is either the inability to bear the cost of debt or the inability to generate timely and sufficient cash flows to pay it back that creates the problem.

If these two things are taken care of, the more one borrows, the greater will be the growth and the higher the profitability.

33. The efficiency trap

Efficiency + Growth = Disaster (if financial intelligence is lacking)

The current assets of a healthy organization should be greater than its current liabilities.

However organizations with high credibility and sterling reputations find vendors willing to sell on longer credit terms and lenders ready to liberally provide short-term loans.

Such organizations must exercise utmost vigilance else they could become victims of what I call the 'efficiency trap'.

Whenever an organization has access to more short-term funds (due to the efficiency of the persons handling the purchase function, who manage to extract the longest credit from vendors) than can be absorbed in short-term avenues (due to the efficiency of the sales people who were able to sell on shorter credit periods), it is natural the excess will get used for long-term purposes (since it is a profitable company always on a growth trajectory, with projects in the pipeline that are hungry for funds).

Such organizations then become guilty of one of the worst crimes of bad finance management, which is to have used short-term funds to finance long-term assets.

34. The single-biggest cause of business failure

If there was a cemetery of failed companies, the tombstones in front of many graves would read, 'Here lies a company that used short-term funds to acquire long-term assets.'

Every entrepreneur must engrave the following message on stone: 'I will never, repeat *never*, use short-term money for long-term purposes', and display it prominently, as a constant reminder.

35. You must know this to take financially smart decisions

Two things entrepreneurs must know about their business in order to take financially intelligent decisions:

1. its cost of capital
2. the variable cost of the product it makes (or the service it provides)

The former will help in taking intelligent capital-investment related decisions and the latter in smart pricing of their products (or services).

36. Requisites for a healthy business from the three financial statements

Section 01

The Balance Sheet

This statement shows the sources and uses of funds.

The long-term sources should be greater than the long-term uses.

The Profit and Loss Statement

This statement reveals incomes and expenses. Expenses can further be broken up, nature-wise, into variable and fixed.

The selling price can, at times, be lower than the total cost, but doesn't matter how desperate the circumstances, it should never be lower than the variable cost.

The Cash Flow Statement

Total cash flow can be divided into that from operations, investing and financing activities.

Cash flow from operations should be positive.

37. Profit vs profiteering

The motive for running a business should be to make profit, and not to profiteer.

Charging excessively high profit margins tantamounts to profiteering.

Generating higher return on investment (RoI) through better financial management increases profit.

Focus on increasing your RoI.

38. An important message for entrepreneurs

Section 01

Never forget, of the various sources used to fund a business, the equity contributed by the owners is the most expensive.

Who is it that usually suffers from the delusion that owners' money is free?

It is often the owners themselves.

I have known so many entrepreneurs who, while evaluating a project, study the cash flow and profitability projections and conclude that 'this project cannot afford borrowed money; so let's invest our own'.

Business owners, please understand, if a project can't afford borrowed funds, it definitely does not deserve your money.

39. Sweat your assets

Lazy assets are the most expensive.

Assets take holidays; liabilities don't.

No banker says, 'Since you don't work on weekends,
you need not pay me interest for those days.'

Convert your non-performing assets to performing ones.
Else get rid of them and release the money.

40. There are two types of NPAs

Non-performing assets can be divided into essential non-performing and non-essential non-performing assets.

The biggest crime is to possess non-essential non-perfoming assets.

41. The worst type of NPA

Cash in hand is a non-performing asset.

Cash beyond what is immediately necessary is a non-essential non-performing asset—the worst kind of asset to possess.

42. Three super secrets of improving profit

1. Optimize your cost of capital by having a judicious mix of cheap (debt) and expensive (equity) money.

2. Improve the proportion of performing vs non-performing assets (convert non-performing assets into performing, or get rid of them and release the money blocked).

3. Sweat your assets more (see that the performing assets perform as long a duration in the year as possible).

43. How much RoI must a business generate

The average cost of capital (including owners' money) in most organizations would be around 20 per cent.

Investment in a business would be justified provided it can earn at least this percentage or higher.

Taking into account that businesses possess non-performing assets and the fact that even the performing assets perform for only about two-thirds of the year, the targeted annualized rate of return jumps up to closer to 50 per cent.

Am I suggesting that you have a 50 per cent profit margin? No. I'm suggesting that the RoI generated should be at least 50 per cent.

44. NPAs are bad for health

Would you ever go to a money lender, borrow a sum of money carrying a rate of interest of 50 per cent, bring that money home, keep it in a cupboard, lock it and sit still for months?

You wouldn't.

If the money is costing you 50 per cent, it better be out working and toiling to earn a minimum of 50 per cent.

It would hurt if it were lying idle in the cupboard.

Folks, if that hurts, why doesn't excess inventory lying in your warehouse hurt as much?

If that hurts, why doesn't overdue money sitting with debtors hurt as much?

If that hurts, why doesn't underutilized capacity of your plant hurt as much?

If that hurts, why doesn't money lying in the bank in a current account hurt as much?

They are all in the same boat.

Never forget that you do not own a single asset that does not have a corresponding liability. And you do not have a single liability that does not have a cost.

Once you understand this, you will perhaps understand one of the biggest secrets of improving profitability.

45. Profit margin vs RoI

Don't start a business unless you can generate a minimum return on investment (RoI) of 40 to 50 per cent.

I'm not speaking of profit margin but RoI.

Even if you earn a profit margin of a mere 2 per cent, but can rotate your money in a fortnight, you would be able to achieve 26 cycles in a year and generate an RoI of 52 per cent.

46. Is there a correlation between profit and money

Company A makes crores in profit and company B is making losses.

Bank statement I reveals crores in the bank and bank statement II shows almost a zero balance.

Can you guess which bank statement belongs to which company?

It is quite possible that the profit-making company does not have money and the company making losses has a hefty bank balance.

Am I saying that the loss-making company has crores in the bank because it is making losses?
No! I am saying that the loss-making company is making losses because it has crores in the bank.

If the company making profit starts hoarding money in the bank, it is a matter of time before it too will stop making profit.

47. Do you understand contribution

The power of compounding has been eulogized often enough, so much so that many, if not most, people understand its significance.

There is another equally wonderful financial concept about which the awareness is not as widespread, and that is **'contribution'**.

Those who appreciate the essence of the term and use it at the right time and in the right situation reap the benefits. Others don't know what they are missing out on.

48. An important word in the costing lexicon

One of the most important words in the dictionary of costing is 'contribution' (which is arrived at by deducting the variable costs from sales).

Sell your product at a loss if need be, but never sell at a negative contribution, no matter how desperate the situation.

If the profit is negative and contribution positive, as volumes grow, the business will eventually make a profit.

But if you ever sell at negative contribution, the more you sell, the bigger will be the loss.

49. A question for you

An airline has a 100 seater aircraft. It fills fuel for $10,000. The per seat fuel cost works out to $100.

In addition, the airline spends another $10 on providing food and a beverage to each flyer. So the total cost per seat is $110.

It decides to price the ticket at $150 to a certain destination.

The airline has managed to sell 50 tickets and the flight is about to take off.

A last-minute passenger, keen to fly but unable to afford the card rate, offers to pay $75.

Should the passenger be accepted? And why?

...continued

Answer:

Yes, the passenger should be accepted.

It is fallacious to say that the cost per seat is $110.

The fuel cost is not $100 per seat. It is $10,000.

The airline will not be filling additional fuel of $100 for this passenger. It has already been filled. It is a sunk cost.

The additional cost for this additional passenger is merely $10. Anything received over and above $10 will result in a positive contribution.

So if the passenger is accepted at $75, then $65 ($75–$10) would be a positive contribution to the airline's bottom line.

50. How much liquid funds must a business possess

Expenses are continuous, while income is sporadic.

Prudence demands that an organization holds adequate cash on hand to be able to meet day-to-day expenses without depending on operational inflows.

A sufficient cash/bank balance is one of the three important components of working capital.

The trick lies in the ability to forecast what constitutes 'sufficient' balance.

If the amount maintained is less than that, it results in inability to meet all the payments due and if it is in excess, it constitutes a non-performing asset, reinforcing my oft-quoted mantra '**less is bad; more is worse**'.

51. Identify 'happy hours' within your organization

Happy hours in a bar is an attempt on the part of the entity running the place to convert 'non-performing hours' into 'performing hours'.

Similarly, in every organization, there are assets which are 'non-performing' either all the time or part of the time.

Strive to convert the non-performing assets into performing assets or get rid of them and release the money blocked in such assets.

Identify happy-hour opportunities within the organization.

This single action can make a significant positive impact on the bottom line.

52. Finance mantras for start-ups to keep in mind

1. Always remember, the objective of running a business is to make profit.

2. A positive bottom line need not be accompanied by a positive bank balance. But timely and sufficient cash flows are essential for the successful running of a business. Enough attention should be paid to the effective management of cash flows.

3. Know your organization's/product's variable cost and the contribution generated per unit. This will help in taking intelligent pricing decisions.

4. Know your cost of capital, which must include the cost of owners' capital

5. *Never* use short-term funds to acquire long-term assets.

6. Maintain a positive liquidity ratio.

53. What is the impact on the bottom line of a change in the top line

Section 01

If in year 1 a company's turnover is 100 and the profit is 20, and in year 2 the sales increases to 200, what will happen to profit?

Will it increase to

1. 40
2. less than 40 or
3. more than 40?

If the profit increases to 40 or less, some heads should roll; it indicates that somebody is bungling up badly.

If the sales of 100 increases to 200, the profit should increase to more than 40.

To how much more than 40 it will increase depends upon the fixed costs in the company's costing structure.

This disproportionate impact on the bottom line due to a certain change in the top line is called the leverage effect.

54. Shorten your working capital cycle

If you wish to increase your profit, try and shorten your working capital cycle.

In a manufacturing organization, this cycle starts with cash. **Cash** gets spent when you buy raw materials and becomes **raw materials inventory** which, when goes into production process, becomes a **finished product**, which when sold gets converted to **debtors** and when you collect money from your customers, it becomes **cash** again.

The cycle is also called the cash-to-cash cycle, and one of the tricks of good finance management is your ability to shorten the cycle.

An organization that holds a raw materials inventory of three months takes another one month to convert it into finished product, and holds on to a finished goods inventory of one month and offers its customers a three-months credit would take about eight months to complete a cycle and achieve one-and-a-half cycles in a year. So a hundred crores invested would probably generate a turnover of a hundred and fifty crores.

...continued

But another organization, which understands my mantra of **'less is bad, more is worse**, holds on to raw materials inventory of one month, maybe takes fifteen days to convert it to finished product by improving its processes, also maintains a finished goods inventory of another fifteen days and, due to better negotiation or maybe a little price reduction, convinces the customers to buy on a one-month credit, would take three months to complete a cycle and achieve four cycles in a year.

A hundred crores invested will bring a turnover of four hundred crores.

People concentrate on increasing selling prices in order to increase profit. Folks, focus instead on shortening your working capital cycle.

55. Are we in business to make profit or to make money

Profit and money are not the same.

Are we in business to make profit or money?

If you choose any one of the above, you are wrong.

Successful businesses are those that make profit *and* generate a positive cash flow.

And both need managing.

That is the crux of good finance management.

The ability to manage profit and the ability to effectively manage cash flow.

56. Finance-management tips for uncertain times

Section 01

1. Avoid fresh debt unless you can see a clear stream of income and timely cash inflows through deployment of the borrowed funds.

2. Outsource wherever possible instead of making in-house.

3. Study all heads of expenses and, where possible, swap fixed costs with variable ones.

57. Will you ever do this in your personal life

Will you ever:

- borrow money at, say, 10 per cent and lend it to somebody at 5 or 7 per cent?
- lend money to somebody who will return it to you after 2 years whereas the source from which you have borrowed it demands it back in 1 year?

You won't do something as foolish as this in your personal life, will you?

Then why do some businesses, among them some of the biggest corporations, do so?

Most problems that businesses face from a financial mismanagement perspective relate to

- either the inability to generate a return on assets that covers the cost of capital used to acquire those assets, or
- the mismatch between the cash inflow from assets and the outflow that has to happen on account of repayment of the corresponding liabilities.

58. 'God is in the details'

'God is in the details', so said Ludwig Mies van der Rohe.

True, no doubt, in many cases, but not while reading balance sheets.

If you wish to read a balance sheet, you will first have to get rid of the clutter.

Else, you will get lost.

59 Do you prepare a funds flow statement

Every organization makes a balance sheet, a profit and loss statement and a cash flow statement, but not everyone prepares a funds flow statement. If you wish to understand the health of your organization better, I would strongly urge you to start doing this regularly. It will help trace where your funds have come from and how these were used, and whether you have been following sound finance-management principles.

60. Finance-management truisms

Here are a few controversial finance-management principles which may go against the grain of common sense unless understood in the right context, and in entirety:

1. Less is bad, more is worse.
2. A characteristic of successful businesses is shortage of cash.
3. Making profit does not mean making money.
4. Higher the fixed cost, greater the profit.
5. Excess bank balance is a sign of worry.
6. You can sell your product at a price lower than its cost and still make a profit, provided you have generated a positive contribution.

61. Do you know of any such bankers

Many businesses get into trouble because they are under-financed. And the reason often is due to the inability to correctly project the requirement of funds, particularly for working-capital needs.

It is understandable that the borrower, often coming from a non-finance background, is unable to do this.

However, the banker, being a finance person, recognizing that the amount will not suffice, should grant a loan of a higher amount.

Do you know of any such bankers? I don't.

But I do know several who sanction an amount lower than what was asked for (which itself was less than the actual need), with a promise to review at a later date to enhance the limits.

I have never understood why this is done.

By starving the borrower of funds, the banker has created the conditions for the business to get into trouble where the ultimate loser is the bank itself.

Section 01

62. What is your excuse for not managing finance

The most common one I hear is: 'It's not my job.'

Since finance management is essentially the taking of financially intelligent decisions/actions, it is everyone's job.

Another excuse used is 'I don't have the time.'

You don't have the time because you are doing many things that should have been handled by others.

I suggest, you take stock of what you do all day.

Make a detailed list of these activities.

Now delegate every activity on the list that you can.

Free yourself to spend time on finance management.

You will reap rich dividends.

63. Doesn't everyone already understand this

I have this tendency of simplifying complicated finance-management principles, and the reaction very often from a listener is, '**Anil, this sounds pretty easy and logical. But you have often said that most business failures happen due to financial mismanagement. Don't people already understand this?**'

My answer is:

1. Yes, they don't.
2. Even if they do, the data to provide this information does not get generated.
3. If the data does get generated, it doesn't get generated on time.
4. If it does get generated on time, it doesn't reach the right people.
5. If it does reach the right people, they don't know what to do with that data.

Unless relevant information gets churned out on time and is provided to the relevant persons, and those people have been trained to read, understand and interpret that data and take suitable action based on it, the organization cannot become financially intelligent.

Section 01

64. Higher inventory results in higher profit

If two companies purchase and sell the same quantity, the one with a higher closing inventory would have made higher profit, because a higher inventory would indicate a lower level of consumption.

This, however, becomes a tool in the hands of unscrupulous people, who inflate inventory when they wish to show higher profit and suppress it when it suits them to show a lower profit.

A well-known oil company, several years ago, had inflated its inventory of oil by about 4 billion barrels, fraudulently inflating profit to the extent of hundreds of billions of dollars, resulting in a surge in the stock price of the company on wall street, only for it to crash when the fraud was eventually revealed.

65. What is internal rate of return

If you invest 100 today at 10 per cent, it will become 110 after 1 year. 110 is the future value of 100 today which can be invested at 10 per cent.

This concept we are taught in school.

Now what is 100? It is the present value (PV) of 110 to be received next year which is discounted at 10 per cent.

So, 100 received next year has a PV of 91, and a hundred received 2 years later has a PV of 83, and three years later, has a PV of 75, and so on.

In this way, you can arrive at the PV of a stream of income to be received in the future as a result of an investment made today.

Let's consider three scenarios.

If you invest 100 today and receive 250 over the next few years, and the PV of 250, applying a discounting factor of 10 per cent*, works out to

a) <100
b) 100
c) >100

(*The discounting factor to be used can be either the earnings expectations from a new project or the opportunity cost of capital.)

...continued

If the present value of the inflows in the future is lesser than 100, it would indicate that the project is earning a rate of return lower than 10 per cent (i.e., the discounting rate applied)

If it is greater than 100, it would indicate that the investment is earning higher than 10 per cent.

And if its discounted cash flow (DCF) is exactly 100, it would indicate that the project is generating a return of 10 per cent.

The rate at which the present value of inflows equals the present value of outflows is called the internal rate of return (IRR).

66. Do you understand the term 'goodwill'

Today, I have two questions for you.

If you see an item called goodwill appearing as an asset on the balance sheet of company X:

Question 1: Whose goodwill does it represent—(a) company X's or (b) someone else's?

Question 2: Is it something (a) good or (b) bad?

In case you have chosen option (a) for both the questions, your answers would be absolutely wrong.

Goodwill is perhaps one of the worst items to appear on a balance sheet and has no resale value.

On your balance sheet, your own goodwill can never appear.

Even if you and your business have a wonderful reputation and command significant goodwill, unless someone is willing to pay you for it, it has no meaning.

...continued

And if you are paid for it, it would be an income and not an asset.

Asset is something you have purchased. So, only if you buy/ acquire somebody else's business and pay an amount over and above the value of the tangible assets that you have received in exchange will it appear as an asset on your balance sheet.

Whose 'goodwill' is appearing on your balance sheet?

It is not yours but of the entity whose business you have acquired.

67. Too much money is a sign of worry

If a business has too much money in the bank, it could be a sign of worry rather than something to be happy about.

One must remember that all money invested in a business has a cost. It is essential that it is deployed into avenues where it generates a return that is higher than what it costs.

Money in the bank is a non-performing asset.
Current accounts don't even earn interest.

Businesses don't make profit by hoarding money. Profit is made by investing the money wisely.

In my opinion, a characteristic of successful businesses is shortage of money.

68. Why businesses fail

Growing too fast, borrowing too much, spreading too thin is never the reason for businesses to go under.

The chief reason almost always is financial mismanagement.

Foolish borrowing, entailing inability to service and to generate sufficient and timely cash flow to repay the loan, funding long-term assets required for expansion with short-term resources are invariably the root causes of business failure.

69. Reserves ≠ Money

Many people, on observing crores appearing under the heading 'reserves and surplus' in a balance sheet, conclude that the company is sitting on crores of bank balance.

One must remember that just as profit and money are not the same, reserves (which represent undistributed profits) are also not the same as money.

Liabilities represent sources of money. Every liability has a corresponding asset. It would be a fallacy to think that a liability in the form of reserves will necessarily be accompanied by an asset in the form of bank balance.

Reserves could be in the form of a building, some equipment or any other asset, and in a rare case also bank balance.

Reserves represent undistributed profit and not unspent money.

70. Do you, at all points of time, know your organization's bottom line

Section 01

If you ask a reasonably senior person from a sales-driven company, 'Do you know your organization's top line?', she will probably tell you the sales achieved till the previous evening.

Sales-driven companies monitor top lines almost on an online basis.

But you now ask the same person, 'Do you also know the bottom line?', chances are, she will not.

Bottom line is usually a black hole.

Often, even business owners do not know whether the organization has made a profit or a loss till the accounts team submits the results.

This I find scary.

Are we in business to generate sales or to make profit? It is the latter.

But we are constantly monitoring the top line and are ignorant of the bottom line.

Scary indeed!

71. When do organizations make real profit

For an organization to make profit, it is not enough that the revenue generated covers the cost of production, the cost of administration, the cost of selling and the cost of borrowed capital.

Unless it also covers (or exceeds) the cost of owners' capital, it cannot be said to have made profit in the real sense of the term.

72. Is your top line going up while the bottom line is coming down

Organizations in expansion mode tend to increase capacities, and then, in an attempt towards utilizing the installed capacities, start selling aggressively.

In their zeal towards procuring fresh business, often orders are accepted on wrong terms (be it on the pricing front, or credit periods).

In such cases, sometimes, the increased sales actually results in reduced profits (of which the sales people are blissfully ignorant, due to their inability to understand the impact on the bottomline of their actions).

If you visit such organizations, you will witness an amazing spurt in activity.

But one must never forget that businesses are run to make profit.

We tend to consider increased levels of busy-ness as progress.

Do not confuse activity with accomplishment. We are not here to generate higher levels of activity.

If the top line is going up and the bottom line is coming down, it is a complete waste of time, energy and resources.

73. How to read a balance sheet

The liabilities in a balance sheet represent sources of money and the assets the uses.

All sources can be broadly divided into two parts: short term and long term (short-term funds being those that need to be returned within one year).

The assets can similarly be classified into short term (those that will get liquidated within one year) and long term.

A healthy balance sheet is one where the long-term funds are greater than long-term uses.

Else, it will indicate that the organization has been financing its long-term assets using short-term funds, which can have seriously detrimental consequences.

Section 01

74. The best investment there is

Till the money is in your purse, it can be stolen. If you pour it into your head, no one can ever take it away from you.

Investment in education gives you the best returns.

Of all the forms of wealth to possess, knowledge figures at the top.

75. Who should take a life insurance policy

Who needs life insurance more—the person who is rich or the one who is poor?

It is the latter.

The logic behind having a life insurance policy is that if, for any reason, the breadwinner of the family is no more, at least so far as the monetary contribution to the family kitty is concerned, the person should not be missed.

When one has accumulated enough assets to leave behind, the requirement for life insurance vanishes. The need for insurance is the greatest when one has yet to amass the desired wealth.

Section 01

76. Finance management in a nutshell

A	Funds raised	➡	B	Funds rrequired
P	Cost at which raised	➡	Q	Rate at which invested
X	Period within which funds have to be returned	➡	Y	Period over which assets will generate the funds

Problem	If $A < B$
Also a problem	If $A > B$
Big problem	If $P > Q$
No problem	If $P < Q$
Big problem	If $X < Y$
No problem	If $X > Y$

77. How should success be measured?

What is your measure of success of a business?
Is it profit?

Perhaps.

How much profit must a business earn to be called a success?

How do you define profit?

Profit is income less expenses.

That means a business should be deemed to be successful when the income generated covers all the costs and leaves behind a surplus.

However, every cost does not appear as an expense in the P&L statement.

Which one doesn't?
The cost of the owners' money

The surplus shown in the P&L should at least cover the cost of the owners' money invested in the business.

But do all owners know what is the cost of their money? You will be surprised how few do.

Many owners consider their money to be free.

78. The power of finance management

Do you know the power of finance management?

- It can transform failing businesses
- It can magnify profits
- It ensures sustainability

Do you know the havoc that bad finance management can cause?

It leads to:

- business failures
- lost jobs
- loan defaults
- corrosion of shareholders' wealth

And for good finance management to prevail, it is not enough that a business has a strong finance department. The entire organization has to be financially intelligent.

It is only when each person is made financially literate, then and only then can an organization become financially intelligent.

79. Immutable laws of finance and business

Ensure:

What you get is more than what you give
(in monetary terms).

What you earn is more than what you spend.
(Either earn more than you spend or spend less than what you earn).

What you have to receive is more than what you need to pay.

If you earn 100 and give alms to a beggar of 150, then the roles will reverse soon.

The employer should earn more than the employee, else the employer will soon be hunting for employment.

A product manufacturer must earn more than the investor in its stocks. Otherwise, the manufacturer will stop manufacturing and become an investor in stocks.

80. Why do I favour productive debt over equity

Section 01

- Debt has an explicit, easily recognizable cost. One can factor it into expenses. One can recognize the need to recover the cost of debt from revenue. Equity on the other hand has an implicit cost which is often not understood; and therefore the need to recover it is also not felt. This is the root cause of most business failures.

- Debt inculcates a sense of responsibility since it comes with the caveat of servicing it—interest plus repayment. There is a difference in the way in which you need to treat debt vs a gift. Debt has to be treated with far greater respect. There is a need to preserve (and not squander) it.

- Debt is cheap.

- Does not dilute control

Anil Lamba on Finance

A series of books on Finance Management

For availability and to learn more about our training programmes, visit us at www.lamconschool.com

Email : training@lamconschool.com
Call : +91. 99 22 351 352

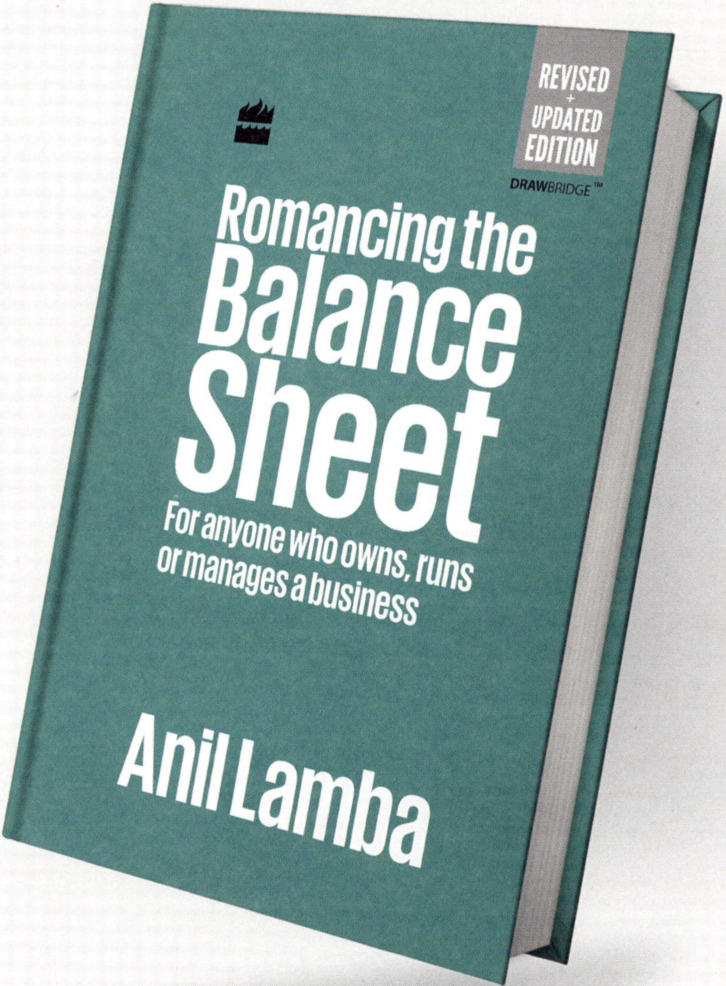
REVISED
+
UPDATED
EDITION
DRAWBRIDGE™
Romancing the
Balance
Sheet
For anyone who owns, runs
or manages a business
Anil Lamba

Accounting

Section 02

01. Bookkeeping followed by the lord

I am quite convinced that even God follows the double entry principle of bookkeeping.

For every debit he puts a corresponding credit in your account.

02. Making vs reading a balance sheet

Section 02

You don't need to know how to make a balance sheet to learn how to read it (just as you don't have to know how to make a motor car to learn how to drive it).

And just because you know how to make it, does not mean you also know how to read it.

Making and reading of balance sheets are two different skill sets.

If you don't learn how to make it, it is okay. But if you don't learn how to read it, you will pay a price.

03. Understand this to learn how to make financial statements

In any organization, all transactions can broadly be categorized into those that bring money in and those that take money out.

If money has come in, it will either be an income or a liability. If it is the former, it appears on the P&L and if the latter, it gets transferred to the balance sheet.

If money has gone out, it will be either an expense or will create an asset—the former goes to the P&L and the latter to the balance sheet.

This understanding will go a long way in helping you learn to make these financial statements and to read them.

Section 02

04. Why is a balance sheet called so

The common perception is that it is called so because its two sides, the liabilities' and the assets' side, are balanced. That is not correct. The reason is something else.

If you make a list of all the account heads, for example, the salaries account, the rent account and the equipment account, you will find in some cases the accounts get written off, the meter starts afresh each year, while in the case of others there is a balance that needs to be carried forward.

For instance, if in year 1, your salary bill was 100 and in year 2 it is 120, how much will be shown against salary in year 2? It will be 120.

On the other hand, if in year 1 you owned a piece of equipment worth 100 and in the following year you have purchased another equipment for 120, how much will be shown against equipment in year 2? It will be 220.

In case of salary, the previous year's figure needs to be written off, whereas in the case of equipment, it gets carried forward.

Those amounts that get written off are transferred to the P&L and those that have a balance to be carried forward appear on the balance sheet.

05. What are expenses and assets from a philosophical point of view

Each penny spent by a business entity needs to be recovered, whether towards payment of salary or acquisition of a building. However all expenditure does not have to be recovered immediately.

There is money spent on certain items which, if spent today, must also be recovered today. Such items are called expenses and are shown on the P&L statement.

There is money spent on other items which too need to be recovered, but you realize that there's no hurry to do so. You don't mind if you recover these over an extended period of time.

When you are willing to stagger the recovery, such items are temporarily called assets and shown on the balance sheet. And each instalment of recovery is called depreciation, which gets recorded as an expense.

A balance sheet is merely a warehouse where you store items till they get transferred to the P&L.

...continued

What needs to be understood is that the ultimate destination of every rupee spent by a business enterprise is the expenses' side of the P&L statement.

Nirvana will only be attained when all the money spent has been shown as expenses in the P&L.

Till this happens, the item on which the money was spent is in a state of animated suspension, which is called an asset.

Anil Lamba on Finance

A series of books on Finance Management

DRAWBRIDGE™
'Monogamy is not a virtue in the stock market. "Flirt with many and marry a few" is the mantra here!'
Flirting with Stocks
Stock Market Investing for Beginners
ANIL LAMBA
BESTSELLING AUTHOR OF
ROMANCING THE BALANCE SHEET

Stock Market Investing

Section 03

01. Safety vs returns

Ask someone who is wanting investment advice, what is more important to you, returns or the safety of your capital? Pat comes the reply, 'safety first'.

People choose investments on grounds of safety when they do not understand anything about safety except its spelling.

Had you asked the best investment advisors in the world in October 2001, what do you think of Enron? Without exception they were all of the opinion that there hasn't been a company like Enron in decades and they were all putting a 'buy' recommendation for the company.

By December 2001, the company did not exist any more.

Three months before the demise of one of the most celebrated companies of the century, if the best brains in the world could not fathom the risk, are you and I qualified to judge safety.

When investments are made on perceptions of safety, safety is never guaranteed, but mediocrity of returns is.

02. Don't buy the scrip if—

Even if you come across a company about which you like everything, before you pick up the phone and call your broker to buy that share, do one little exercise.

Go back a few quarters and plot a sales graph of the company. Unless the graph is looking towards the sky, I suggest don't buy that share.

There are thousands of scrips to choose from.
Why would you want to go out of your way and buy the shares of a company whose sales is either stagnating or has started falling?

03. How to select a fundamentally sound company to invest in

Study the financial data for the last few quarters
and ensure these five criteria are satisfied:

1. The **sales** is consistently on the rise.

2. The **gross profit** is increasing at least at the same pace as the increase in sales.

3. The **net profit** is increasing at a pace faster than the increase in sales.

4. The **earnings** per share is higher than the industry average.

5. The **price-to-earnings** ratio is lower than the industry average.

04. Investing in stocks is a national duty

When a large percentage of the population invests in shares, the stock market is teeming with activity, and anyone who wishes to buy can find a seller, and vice versa.

When buyers and sellers can easily locate each other, it provides an assured exit route for the investors, and more people are willing to invest in businesses.

Entrepreneurs then find it easier to raise money, which in turn leads to more enterprise, more GDP growth, more employment, more tax collection et al.

And all this started because you and I decided that we should invest in shares.

05. These phrases have no place while investing

Two phrases don't exist in the stock market lexicon:

1. Maximum profit
2. Minimum loss

Section 03

06. Stock market investing: rules

Keep profits open-ended and put a stop-loss.

Most people tend to do the reverse; they put a limit on profit and keep losses open-ended.

07. Rules for buying and selling

Never buy in a falling market.
Never sell in a rising market.

Buy at the beginning of the rising trend.
Sell at the beginning of the falling phase.

Learn the art of technical analysis.

Section 03

08. Producers must earn more than investors

It is essential that the product maker earns more than the investor in its stocks.

If one makes more money buying and selling Bajaj Auto shares than the Bajaj family does making and selling Bajaj motorcycles, sooner or later they themselves will stop making bikes and start investing in shares.

That is when the problem starts.

09. How many scrips should your portfolio have

The number of scrips in your stock portfolio should preferably be in single digit. You certainly should not invest all your investible surplus in one stock, but distributing it over too many also makes it unwieldy.

'Put all your eggs in one basket and watch the damn basket (apologies to Mark Twain)' should be the mantra, if you get my drift.

10. You should be polygamous here

Section 03

Monogamy is not a virtue in the share market.

Flirt with many and marry a few is the mantra while investing in stocks.

Anil Lamba on Finance

A series of books on Finance Management

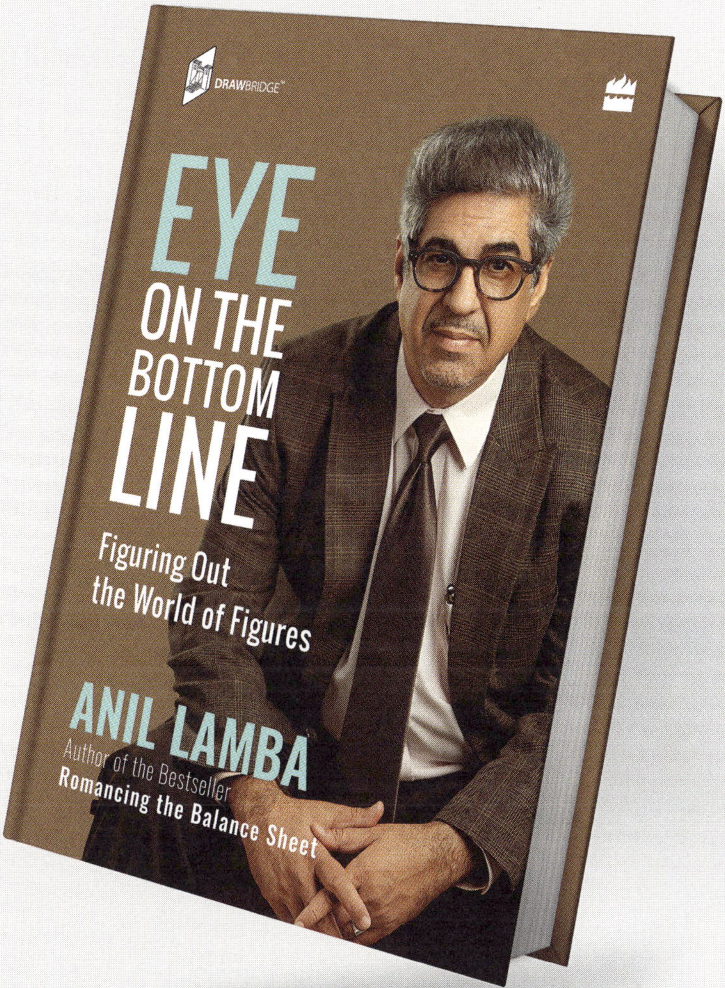
DRAWBRIDGE
EYE
ON THE
BOTTOM
LINE
Figuring Out
the World of Figures
ANIL LAMBA
Author of the Bestseller
Romancing the Balance Sheet

Income Tax

Section 04

01. Income tax: the flip side

Very often you read articles painting a dismal picture of the ridiculously low percentage of our population that pays income tax.

Let me today show you a brighter side.

When you earn a rupee, you pay income tax.

Let's say, you've been waiting to earn some money so you can buy a shirt.

When you do so, it becomes the shirt seller's income, who will pay income tax on the same rupee again.

When the shirt seller spends it to buy a pair of shoes, it becomes the shoe seller's income, who again pays income tax.

Do you realize, each time a rupee merely changes hands, it becomes somebody's income and the government gets a share of that?

Someone had worked out that for every rupee that is printed, more than 97 paise go back to the government in the form of income tax alone.

Section 04

02. The lesser pain theory

Pain is inevitable. Payment of income tax hurts. The consequences of non-payment also hurt.

A person will pay so long as the pain of payment is lesser than the pain of the consequences of not paying.

So when governments raise taxes, for a while tax collection goes up. Then a threshold rate is reached. Beyond this level an increase in the rate of taxes has a counter effect, since the pain of paying is greater than the fear and penalties of default.

This threshold rate is the optimum rate of tax, identification of which is often a matter of trial and error.

03. Should people earning through illegal means pay income tax

Should a thief pay income tax on his earnings?
Should a smuggler pay tax on his income?
Should a person making money through illegal means pay income tax on his wages of sin?

Or maybe I should phrase this differently.

Is a thief supposed to pay income tax on his earnings; does a smuggler have to pay tax on his income; should a person making money through illegal means be paying income tax on his wages of sin?

Does the money made by all the above constitute income as envisaged by the income tax act?

The answer to this question lies in asking another question.
Is the levy of income tax an honour bestowed by the government? Or is it something that pinches and hurts?

Let's face it, it hurts.

I don't know a single person who when asked to pay tax let's out a hoot of joy and on doling out the sum gets a warm feeling in his bosom that comes from the satisfaction of having performed one's national duty.

...continued

Section 04

Visualize these two scenarios :

1. Government speaking with individual A and saying 'Since you are an honest person who is earning money through hard work and toil and running a legitimate activity, I will honour you by taking 20–30 per cent of your income as income tax.'

2. Government speaking with individual B, a dishonest person who earns money through illegal means using skullduggery, saying 'I'm going to punish you by not taking any income tax from you.'

If paying tax hurts the payer, does it make sense, inflicting this pain on the honest earner of income and exempting the dishonest person from payment of tax?

Of course, illegal income and that earned through dishonest means is also taxable.

04. Voluntary disclosure schemes

Not spending is a bigger evil than tax evasion.

Voluntary disclosure schemes announced by governments are poignant appeals to tax evaders beseeching them to start spending, even if tax has not been paid on the money earned.

And in case they are scared of the consequences, the government assures no action will be taken.

05. Can illegal income be white

Can illegal income be white?
Can legal income be black?

Black or white has nothing to do with how the income was acquired. It simply depends on whether income-tax was paid or not.

If a smuggler gets caught and income-tax is collected on the earnings from the sale of the smuggled goods, that income would be white.

And if a person earns through honest means but does not pay income tax, the income would be deemed to be black.

06. Tax evasion has a cost

Any attempt at saving income tax is perhaps more expensive than the payment of tax itself.

And tax evasion is the most expensive of all.

Section 04

Anil Lamba on Finance

A series of books on Finance Management

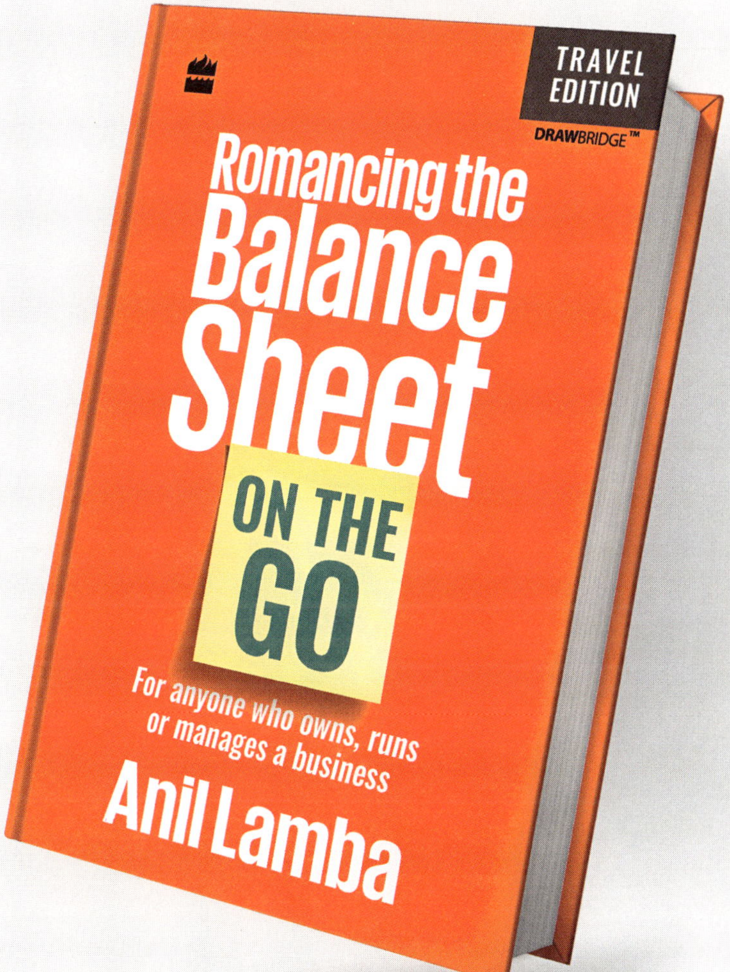
TRAVEL
EDITION
DRAWBRIDGE™
Romancing the
Balance
Sheet
ON THE
GO
For anyone who owns, runs
or manages a business
Anil Lamba

Macro Economics

Section 05

01. Who is responsible for recession

To understand this, we must first understand the economic circle.

The population of a country constitutes its labour force.

The *productivity* of the labour creates the supply of goods and services in a country.

Wages paid to the workers are the reward for productivity.

The wages create the buying power to spend, resulting in *demand* for goods and services.

This demand mops up the supply.

And the circle gets completed.

Pay your workers liberally.
If you don't, where will they get the money from to spend and buy what you have made?

When wages do not keep pace with productivity, the demand falls short of supply.

By not paying enough, entrepreneurs themselves sow the seeds of recession.

Section 05

02. Debt-to-GDP measures the financial leverage of an economy

If a country's debt-GDP ratio is greater than 100 per cent, it indicates that the borrowings are in excess of the value of total goods and services produced by the nation.

It also indicates an inability to service the debt, leading to a fall in ratings and consequent difficulty in taking further loans, which would come at higher interest.

Venezuela has the highest debt-GDP ratio at 350 per cent.
Japan occupies the second slot with a ratio of 266 per cent.
USA stands at number 12, with a ratio of 128 per cent.
India has a healthy ratio of 69.62 per cent.

03. The government's budget

Governments make budgets (a plan showing where the money will come from and how it will be spent) and so do many of us.

What's the difference between the two?

You and I will first try and estimate how much we can receive and, based on that, plan the expenditure.

Governments work in the reverse. They first decide the expenditure and then take care of minor details of where this money will come from.

I often get the feeling that there are two separate groups at work—one planning the spending and the other in-charge of raising the money—and the two are not on talking terms with each other.

And if these two groups work independently of one another, then we can visualize three situations that can arise.

1. The money planned to be raised matches the amount of planned expenditure, in which case it will be called a '**balanced budget' (I have not seen one so far)**.

...continued

2. The amount to be received is greater than what is to be spent—called a '**surplus budget**' **(never seen one either)**.

3. The expenditure is greater than the receipts—'**deficit budget**' **(which is the what we see happening year after year).**

A deficit budget essentially means that the collections are 100 and the expenditure is, say, 120. You and I cannot do this, but governments can, since they also happen to own the printing press.

When governments print money to spend, this phenomenon is called deficit financing.

04. What causes inflation

When governments print money to spend, the fallout is inflation.

What is the connection?

Just because the government printed money, why did the bread in the bakery become more expensive?

Inflation is a result of demand exceeding supply.

If every individual in a country starts working twice as hard, and earns twice as much as before, the buying power of the entire nation would have doubled.

Will it lead to a rise in prices?

The answer is, no, since the higher earnings are a result of people having worked harder which would also have positively impacted the supply of goods and services.

However, when governments print money to spend, there is merely an increase in the supply of money without a corresponding increase in the quantity of goods, and therefore it becomes inflationary.

More money is now chasing the same quantity of goods.

05. Demand, supply and price

Section 05

When the supply of a commodity exceeds its demand, the price will tend to fall to a level where it will attract a buyer.

When the demand for a commodity exceeds its supply, the price will tend to rise to a level where it will eventually induce a holder of that commodity to part with it.

This works as much in the vegetable market as in the stock market.

06. Problems of developed nations

Most problems faced by developing countries are related to **shortages**—demand usually outstrips supply.

Developed economies, on the other hand, have problems of **surpluses**.

Due to advancement in technology and higher productivity of machines and human resources, they end up producing far in excess of what they can consume.

And what do they do with the surplus? After all attempts at getting rid of the excess are exhausted, they throw it into the sea.

There are countries that throw tonnes of food grains into the sea and spend billions of dollars each year on incentives given to farmers if they agree not to grow anything on their land.

Section 05

07. What is a debt trap

Despite the fact that governments borrow at very low rates of interest, there are instances where a country's interest payments exceed the amount of borrowings in a particular year. **How does this happen?**

Let's imagine that many years back a country borrowed 100 and paid, let's say, 2 as interest.

The following year it borrowed another 100 (but forgot to return the earlier loan) and paid 4 as interest.

Soon it was borrowing 100 and paying interest of 100.

And then came a stage where it was borrowing 100 and paying 150 by way of interest.

When a country (or anyone) is forced to borrow in order to pay interest on earlier borrowings, that situation is called a debt trap.

08. Money supply vs supply of goods and services

For prices to remain steady, the money supply should grow commensurate with the increase in the supply of goods and services.

If the supply of goods and services grows faster, prices will fall.

If the increase in money supply is greater, it will cause inflation, which in turn will eventually lead to an increase in interest rates which, if not handled well, can result in recession.

09. USD: the world's reserve currency

If a country's domestic spending exceeds its receipts, it can print money to meet the shortfall (deficit financing). But if its imports exceed its exports, it cannot resort to printing since for international spending you need dollars (which is the world's reserve currency, a status bestowed upon it in 1944 at the Bretton Woods Conference).

However, the USA can print dollars, and it does, with reckless abandon.

One shudders to think what will happen to the USA in case the dollar ever loses the reserve currency status.

Anil Lamba on Finance

A series of books on Finance Management

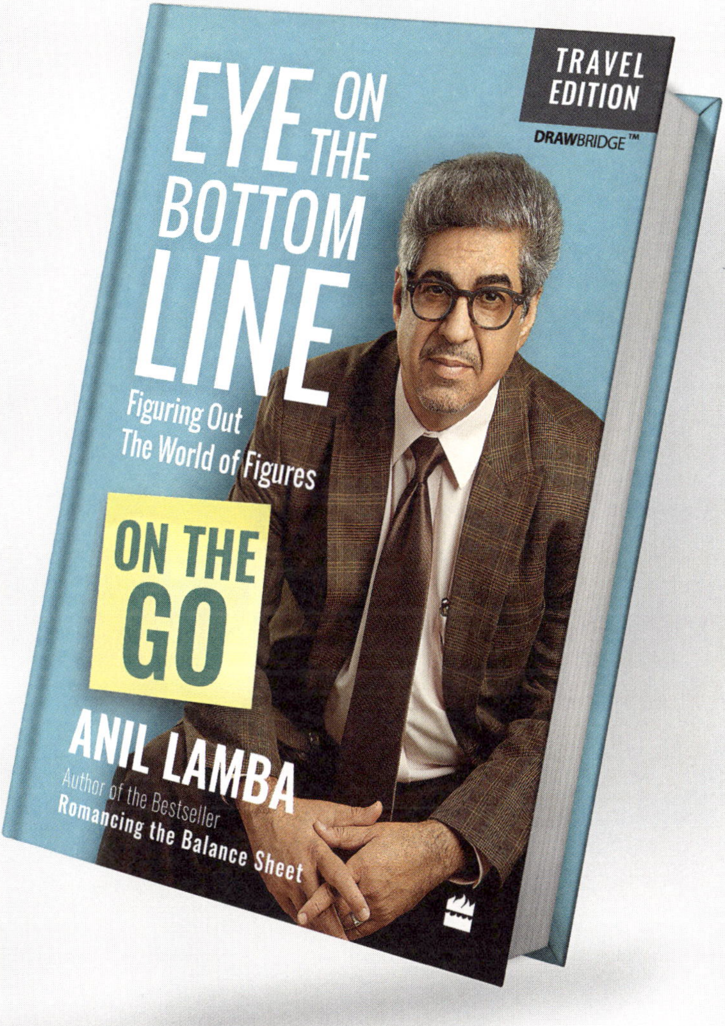
TRAVEL EDITION
DRAWBRIDGE™
EYE ON THE BOTTOM LINE
Figuring Out The World of Figures
ON THE GO
ANIL LAMBA
Author of the Bestseller
Romancing the Balance Sheet

Shorts

Small in size but packing a heavy punch

Section 06

01.

Financial knowledge is a powerful weapon.

Are you armed?

02.

When the going gets tough, **only the financially intelligent survive**.

03.

If the finance management foundation of your business is weak, **the structure that you build on it will eventually collapse**.

04.

Show me an individual who says
'I am a non-finance person'
and I will show you one who is
headed towards financial trouble.

05.

Strive not to maximize profit.

Strive to maximize ROI instead.

06.

06 Section

A penny saved is a penny wasted.

A penny invested can build you a fortune.

07.

Profit has many relatives.

Loss is an orphan.

08.

If you think financial education is expensive, **you haven't understood the cost of financial ignorance**.

09.

When corporate managements announce
'We are a debt-free company',
I have never understood whether they are boasting or apologizing.

Section 06

10.

Good finance management alone cannot make a business successful, **but bad finance management can single-handedly destroy it**.

11.

A business that is unable to bear the cost of borrowed funds **certainly can't afford the cost of equity**.

12.

Amongst the more important skills in an entrepreneur's repertoire **is the ability to speak, interact and dance with numbers**.

13.

It takes guts to start a business **and financial acumen to make a success of it**.

14.

Section 06

Productive borrowing facilitates accelerated growth.

Non-productive debt causes business failures.

Borrow sensibly.

15.

Generating top line is a means towards achieving an end.

And the end is to have a decent, healthy bottom line.

16.

Section 06

Be nice to finance professionals.

They are financial doctors and can save your life.

17.

You may spend a lifetime not knowing how to make a balance sheet, and it's no big deal.
But if you don't learn how to read a balance sheet, you will pay a price for this ignorance.

Section 06

18.

Losses by design are acceptable;
profits by default are not.

19.

Businesses don't die.

They are killed by financially illiterate entrepreneurs and employees.

20.

Your level of success in life depends on your level of financial intelligence.

About the Author

Dr Anil Lamba is a bestselling author, financial literacy activist and international corporate trainer. A chartered accountant with degrees in commence and law as well as a doctorate in taxation, his training programmes are held internationally. Dr Lamba's client list exceeds three thousand large- and medium-sized corporations spread across India, the US, Europe, Russia, Africa, West Asia and the Far East.

HarperCollins *Publishers* India

At HarperCollins India, we believe in telling the best stories and finding the widest readership for our books in every format possible. We started publishing in 1992; a great deal has changed since then, but what has remained constant is the passion with which our authors write their books, the love with which readers receive them, and the sheer joy and excitement that we as publishers feel in being a part of the publishing process.

Over the years, we've had the pleasure of publishing some of the finest writing from the subcontinent and around the world, including several award-winning titles and some of the biggest bestsellers in India's publishing history. But nothing has meant more to us than the fact that millions of people have read the books we published, and that somewhere, a book of ours might have made a difference.

As we look to the future, we go back to that one word—a word which has been a driving force for us all these years.

Read.

Harper Collins 4th HARPER FICTION HARPER NON-FICTION HARPER BUSINESS HarperCollins *Children's Books*

HARPER DESIGN Harper Sport HARPER PERENNIAL HARPER VANTAGE हार्पर हिन्दी